BACH
THE CONFLICT BETWEEN THE
SACRED AND THE SECULAR

Da Capo Press Music Reprint Series

BACH
THE CONFLICT BETWEEN THE SACRED AND THE SECULAR

By Leo Schrade

Da Capo Press • New York • 1973

Library of Congress Cataloging in Publication Data

Schrade, Leo, 1903-1964.
  Bach.

  (Da Capo Press music reprint series)
  Reprint of the ed. published by Merlin Press, New
York, which was reprinted from the Journal of the
history of ideas, v. 7, no. 2., Apr. 1946, and issued
as v. 1 of Merlin music books.
  1. Bach, Johann Sebastian, 1685-1750.   I. Title.
[ML410.B1S27   1973]   780'.92'4   73-4331
ISBN 0-306-70581-8

This Da Capo Press edition of *Bach, the Conflict Between the Sacred and the Secular* is an unabridged republication of the 1955 edition published in New York.

Published by Da Capo Press, Inc.
A Subsidiary of Plenum Publishing Corporation
227 West 17th Street, New York, N.Y. 10011

BACH
THE CONFLICT BETWEEN THE
SACRED AND THE SECULAR

BACH

THE CONFLICT
BETWEEN
THE SACRED
AND
THE SECULAR

LEO SCHRADE

MERLIN PRESS · NEW YORK

Printed in Germany

THIS IS A MERLIN PRESS BOOK

Designed by Milton J. Goodman

OF THIS EDITION ONLY FIFTEEN HUNDRED
COPIES WERE MADE

THIS IS NUMBER _____

UNDERSTANDING AND esteem for Bach's music have developed in a way not altogether regular. The course of men's appreciation of Bach has moved back and forth, like the tides. The causes that have set these tides in motion have changed from time to time. Hence we always think we are "discovering" Bach anew. If signs are not wholly deceptive, a new wave seems to be rising here and now. A new historical interpretation may therefore be worth while.

Whenever in the past historical explanation has claimed to reveal the most ultimate and profound secrets of Bach's music, it has been only in the most general terms that the scholar, the historian, the philosophical interpreter have been able to fathom the depths of his work. Its sum and substance have been held to consist in the force of its religious quality, its spiritual power, its profundity of feeling, its abundance of humanity. We accept these terms as entirely appropriate. It seems that all who have a mind for his music draw upon such a terminology to express the ultimate and inexplicable. Such words are nebulous, and always exposed to danger; they are apt to be vague and empty. Their meaning as applied to Bach becomes clear in the light of his own historical context. Was religious quality or intensity of feeling in fact the historical import of Bach and his

4

work? And if so, was it the real force that gave his work its form? If Bach spoke the language of religion, of human depth and feeling, we must learn to understand its significance in terms of his own situation and problems, or else it merely calls forth our subjective and uncontrolled imagination. This is the true task of historical interpretation.

The domestic steadiness resulting from his social station as a burgher is probably the most striking, at any rate the most obvious, trait of Bach's life. It characterized all his kinfolk far and near. The Bachs lived for generations scattered over Thuringia and Saxony; they remained there. But despite the stout gravity of such an existence, Johann Sebastian Bach evinced throughout his life a peculiar restlessness, an anxiety hard to understand, and not in conformity with his usual firmness and composure. We are not referring to those sudden explosions of irascibility of which various stories are related. We mean the restlessness of the artist.

Wherever he resided, this perturbed state of mind in matters of art never left him. Continual search is a prominent characteristic of his musicianship. He had no apparent plan, but rushed uneasily from one artistic discovery to another. This may have been nothing more than an accidental and quite natural way of exploring local traditions wherever he happened to be staying. But these discoveries were more than chance encounters. They spring from the ideal he early conceived for his art; they derive from the goal he put definitely into words. To pursue this goal was his life-work, and it was this vocation that filled him with restlessness. It is at this point that we feel the historical tenseness of Bach's situation arising, it is in this sense that we must take his religious feeling as an historical phenomenon. Bach's artistic search grew out of the goal he set himself. In order to acquire the power to pursue it appropriately he moved about and absorbed all the music he could find.

The state of music he encountered was utterly confusing. Germany had no distinctive style of its own. It was Italy that set forth the dominating style of the baroque age. Because of this uncertainty about the prevailing musical style, a style which had its home outside his own country, and because of the necessity his goal laid upon him to search for all possible expressions and forms, the tension that runs through Bach's life seems to have arisen from the conditions of his times and not to be altogether personal. Musicians not in the most intimate contact with the center of style are exposed to the influence of all sorts of traditions;

they will always search restlessly until they find that source. If such is the lot of truly great composers their fate becomes tragic. It is a situation with which it is of no avail to quarrel, but which again and again challenges the very great to revolt. Händel went to Italy after having fully experienced the perplexing musical state of Germany. Bach remained there.

This was likewise the result of necessity, and not of individual predilection. It was destiny that forced Bach into the position of a German organist and cantor, and consequently into all the narrow and limited forms of life that went with that position. In saying "destiny," we mean his goal, his vocation. Bach himself first described it in a document that is probably the most important of all the extant sources for understanding his aims. When in 1708 he submitted his resignation to the municipal council of Mühlhausen, at the age of twenty-three, he offered significant reasons. "Although it was my intention to advance the music in the divine service toward its very end and purpose (**Endzweck**), a regulated church music in honor of God; although it was also my intention here to improve the church music, which in nearly all villages is on the increase and is often better treated than here; although for the purpose of improvement I provided, not without expense, a good supply of the best selected church compositions, and also, in observation of my duty, submitted a project for the repair of the unsatisfactory and damaged organ, and, in short, would have fulfilled my obligations with enthusiasm: it so happened that none of this was possible without vexatious relations. . . . So God willed to bring about an opportunity that will not only put me in a better position so far as the subsistence of my livelihood is concerned, but will also make it possible for me, without annoyance to others, **to persevere in working for my very end which consists in organizing church music well.**"

Here for the first time Bach lays down the direction in which his work must grow. He characterizes the vocation in which he must serve all his life; his view of the goal is unusually clear and his will to pursue it unusually determined. His art is directed toward organizing church music, toward regulating it well to the honor of God. From this it has been concluded that Bach had a personal inclination toward and liking for sacred music—as though ends of this character have ever been the result of the individual's likes and dislikes! We may have forgotten that religion and the service it demands go far beyond the dispositions and inclinations of the individual; the obligations involved do not spring altogether from the "free" will of man. No "liberal" propensity called forth Bach's decision. The document of Mühlhausen becomes, indeed, one of the historic landmarks, its significance reaching out far beyond the personal development of Bach. Yet even from the individual point of view it is remarkable that a young man of twenty-three should set before himself, in full clarity and unrestrained determination, the goal of his life-work.

Bach's aim, then, is unusual in his time and of momentous consequence for him. His generation did not see church music as the one and exclusive form the art should or could have, to say nothing of the reform and reorganization which Bach held to be a necessity. It is true that Bach's inferiors if appointed church musicians—and most of them were—fulfilled their duties by placing traditional

11

music in the service. There is no "end," no idea, not even a particular merit in disposing of duties such as fall to the musician's daily routine. Bach, however, brings in the idea of reform; he conceives of a new and inspiring aim; he intends to impart to church music a new structure. Such reforms are not invented because a person likes to invent them. On the contrary, an idea brings the reform to life; in this case it was the Lutheran idea of the Protestant church. Bach visualized a new regulation of religious life through music, a "birth of the Church out of the spirit of music," to give a famous expression a new turn.

The Mühlhausen document marks the last great moment of German baroque music. Almost at the same time Händel was definitely turning away from German musical conditions and toward the opera, as the ultimate opportunity for the artist to attain world fame and representative power. Bach dedicated himself to sacred music as the final opportunity to give expression to religion bound up with the church. Both Händel and Bach showed a mysterious assurance of decision; nearly all their further steps were but consequences once the decision had been made.

Bach accepted his work as of divine origin, as his vocation, not because of any individual inclination and not even because of personal piety, but in full recognition of the idea Luther had conceived of the church. So the whole musicianship of Bach obtains its meaning from his aim, which casts light upon all he did and worked for, against which any personal expression of life for its own sake fell back into insignificance. The determination of Bach, his assurance in approaching his work, his inner restlessness and continual search for artistic experience, all this derives from the grace of the vocation bestowed upon him as the medium through which to symbolize the idea of the church, faith, religion in his music. The process of development now to be unfolded, the advance Bach made in bringing the task into reality, reveals this destiny fully.

ACH SPENT HIS EARLY years from 1685 to 1700, at Eisenach and Ohrdruf. The entire musical life was there organized around the municipality. Since the Reformation German music had drawn all its substance from the city. Musical compositions had to be furnished for all civic and religious events in the town. Training in music was carried on by the school as well as by the church, and the same persons often served in both places. In consequence of this unifying

15

process, exemplified in the **"Kantorei,"** a musical institution most prominent during the age of the Reformation, the repertory of musical works in any one city was to an astonishing degree of one kind only—all alike. But this organization limited the effectiveness and activity of the musician to the single city in which he lived, regardless of the artistic greatness he might have achieved. There were elaborate rules which forbade any activity outside the town. Although a sort of illegal practice existed, such practice did not pay, as the delinquent musicians who lent their services to neighboring cities or villages had to expect severe punishment. The influence of this musical activity usually did not extend far beyond the range of view the church tower afforded. This extreme limitation is significant for the whole of German baroque music. We must keep this always in mind if we are to understand the calamities that befell the greatest of the German musicians during that period, not as personal misfortunes that call for sympathy, but as their inevitable historical destiny. Heinrich Schütz suffered severely from such limitations and narrow circumstances. Händel cast them off; he left all the institutions of the city and turned once and for all to the opera which granted wider scope.

Bach, however, grew up and remained in the small-town atmosphere and narrowness. Eisenach and Ohrdruf gave him his first experience of this type of music organization. But Ohrdruf had an additional significance. Although a very small place, it exposed Bach to influences the importance of which increased to proportions far beyond the size of the town. Strangely enough, problems significant for his artistic advancement also appear

17

for the first time. Some decision with regard to his future course can be seen gradually taking form. Still more strangely, a great many essential traits begin to make their appearance at Ohrdruf; their significance will later increase. It is of extreme importance that at Ohrdruf Bach, though but a boy, came in contact with a religious movement that seemingly had no direct bearing on his music, but nonetheless was to accumulate considerable weight since it influenced his professional position. Ohrdruf brought home the first experience with Pietism. This religious movement had long had a firm hold on Ohrdruf. The opposition between the orthodox and the Pietistic course seems to have been especially vehement there; any small town may give divergent opinions a greater violence of expression than the large city, where disunion is more readily covered up. Ohr-

[handwritten marginal note: stressed personal piety o[ver] religious formali[ty] & ortho...]

druf was such a stronghold of Pietism as to gain the dubious distinction of harboring even disreputable extremists who did great harm to the movement as a whole; and it is said that "zealots, seceders from other regions, found shelter" there.

The authorities of the school Bach attended were violently opposed to Pietism; in the most determined manner they uncompromisingly upheld the orthodox point of view. Every teacher of the school or officer of the town had, upon appointment, to take the oath on the so-called **formulae concordantiae** of the orthodox church; the signature established the procedure. Bach's brother, Johann Christoph, had also signed the orthodox formulae. Some letters by Christoph Kiesewetter, who had been since 1696 rector of the school Bach attended, give a very lively and instructive picture of Pietism at Ohrdruf; they portray the

19

situation in the first decade of the eighteenth century.[1] We do not know in what way Bach, fifteen years old, may have taken part in the movement. That this schism which divided the whole community into two camps should have left him unimpressed it is impossible to think. On the contrary, we must assume that Pietism began to affect his religious thought fundamentally; later he possessed in his own library all the important literature of the Pietistic theologians. A religious experience appears side by side with his artistic beginnings. This much at least we must grant, that the period of Ohrdruf determined many of Bach's further steps.

It was then that the time of tension

[1] Here we should mention a publication, important for the subject, but—so far as we can see—hitherto overlooked; Theodor Wotschke: "Der Pietismus in Thüringen," in *Thüringisch-Sächsische Zeitschrift für Geschichte und Kunst*, vol. 18 (Halle, 1929).

and restlessness began. An uncertainty
with regard to the true character of musical style as well as to the whole state of
music in Germany must have entered his
mind. Not many years had passed since
Heinrich Schütz had surveyed—at the
end of his life—the state of German music; he had expressed many a word of des-
pair and resignation, most frequently in
his letters; he then no longer believed
that his old ideal could be realized, of
giving German music a unity of both
style and repertory. The condition Schütz
had often described in tragic tones had
not changed, either for the better or for
the worse, until the time when Bach was
on the verge of an important period. The
musical traditions of the Bach family, his
growing up in a small town, the type of
training he obtained, all this allowed him
little "free choice." Had he been given
such a free choice, and had his view not

been obstructed by the limitations of his early days, his preference might have turned to Italy, as Schütz in the past had gone south to search for the "true" musical style, as Händel was to go to Italy as the very source of the baroque opera. But Bach was heir to the traditions of a long line of ancestors who had all been musicians of the town's **Kantorei,** or organists. Training in their schools and his own excellent skill as organist were good enough reasons for continuing the work of his forefathers. To improve his skill in organ music Bach quite naturally turned his attention to the German North, where this branch of music was of high standing as regards both playing and composition. It possessed sufficient originality to differ distinctly from the organ music of the German South or from Italian music.

Bach came to Lüneburg in 1700, at the

age of fifteen. Here, however, all that the German **Kantorei** stood for in traditional training as well as in the manner of composition made itself felt. Here any musician must have been exposed to the heavy impact of the most confusing influences. When a young composer came with the intention of getting a clear idea of what style in composition in his day should be, clarity was the last thing he could find. The repertory of the vocal music used at Lüneburg while Bach was a singer in the choir gives full evidence of the complete lack of any uniformity. And this, indeed, is very characteristic of the situation in which during the baroque period we find the **Kantorei,** an institution that had fulfilled its true function during the epoch of Dutch composition, from about 1450 to 1600, and in Germany especially during the age of the Reformation. Now the choral repertory of Lüne-

23

burg was in complete disorder. The names of the composers tell a confused story; they are: Aichinger, De Monte, Gabrieli, Gallus, Gastoldi, Grandi, Hammerschmidt, Ingegneri, Josquin, Adam Krieger, Lassus, Marenzio, Merulo, Monteverdi, Palestrina, Praetorius, Schop, Selle, Senfl, Vecchi, and Viadana. In terms of musical style there were a good many Dutch compositions, but without any discrimination; all the shades of the Dutch style are represented, with the exception of its oldest type, that of Ockeghem; and also works of the same school that show distinctly the process of stylistic disintegration. In addition, the baroque style of the solo song as well as of the concerto was taken up. The Obsequies and Sacred Concerts of Heinrich Schütz were perhaps also part of the Lüneburg repertory. The accomplishments of not less than two centuries, from 1500 to 1700, were combined into the strangest mixture, entirely without order, without the slightest attempt to distinguish the different compositions by periods or countries. We must not assume, as has been done, that the old compositions were sung for any reason of "historical" interest, as we might be concerned with "the music of old." The obsolete works were **still** sung, and purely on the strength of the tradition in the **Kantorei;** when the more recent compositions began to be circulated, they were taken up as they became known and grafted upon the old stock. Consequently, the German baroque musician was confronted with an inheritance of spiritual power drawn from previous centuries. The musical service performed by the cantor afforded no clear view into the actual state of contemporary music. Bach met precisely this situation when he started at Lüneburg. From

25

this, historians have concluded that such a vast repertory offered a rare opportunity to study musical composition on a really large scale, since it led the musician back to the technique of times past, even as early as 1500. The conclusion is unintelligent and unhistorical. In so far as the German baroque musicians were at all aware of the state of things, they suffered seriously from that grand scale, and it is we who have slighted the fateful consequences that arose from this situation.

Bach was on the quest, and his inquiries were answered by ancient and disorderly traditions, by a complex assortment of styles. Remote and recent epochs spoke to him at one and the same time with entirely different forms of expression. It was for this reason that the restlessness of the artist in dire uncertainty came over Bach and long remained with him. Lüneburg and the study of its choral music did not satisfy him. Bach explored at the same time the art of Loewe, whose work had no relation to the vocal tradition of the choir in which he was singing. He also studied the work of Böhm thoroughly. His early training in organ music called for further intensification of his knowledge in this field, and so he went to Hamburg to learn from Reinken. The musical repertory at the court of Celle, not far from Lüneburg, showed peculiar characteristics; hence it became an additional point of attraction. The ambitious miniature imitations of Versailles exposed the German baroque courts to the influences of French music. It was for this French character that Bach went to Celle. The stay at Lüneburg was also a constant turning about; with steadfast purpose Bach exploited all he could reach in the neighborhood. Characteristic of a development that proceeds without any certain guide, Bach took with greater seriousness the works he became successively acquainted with and attributed to them greater significance than most of them were entitled to, if viewed in the light of the whole musical achievement of the period. They turned out to be more than a momentary stimulus to his creative power. This, too, is significant. The models he encountered made their unmerited importance felt to the exclusion of anything else because there was nothing in sight that could adjust this relative experience to the "absolute" whole. Bach was in no real touch with the artistic vitality that always prevails in the center of style and carries everything before it, small and great alike. While during the period at Lüneburg he was steadily exploring the "true" state of music, whatever "truth" there was available, he perceived only what interested

him as the future cantor and organist.
Perhaps these are the most restless years
in his life. It explains nothing, however,
to attribute this to youth's insatiable
thirst for knowledge. Bach stayed only
two and a half years at Lüneburg; but
despite its brevity the period brought him
experience with the vocal music of the
sixteenth and seventeenth centuries, with
the works of Loewe, Böhm, Reinken, and
the French baroque music. Indeed, they
show an unusual diversity.

Bach was determined to begin his musical life as a cantor and organist. This his
trips to Reinken in Hamburg make quite
apparent. Not for a moment did he think
of turning to Reinhard Keiser, the composer of operas. Hamburg was perhaps
the only city in baroque Germany which
through its opera afforded in a scope greater than usual and in splendid execution,
a relatively adequate idea of baroque mu-

29

sic. The plan to unite the prevailing Italian opera with the forms of the French court, the goal of Kusser, and to create out of such a unification a distinctive German opera on the grandiose scale of baroque man, the idea of Keiser, produced an achievement astonishingly close to the magnificent gesture with which the prominent men of the time showed themselves masters of their art. Through these works Hamburg became the only city where the narrowness of German musical conditions had been overcome. And on this point, all the differences of inner structure are brought out that separate Händel and Bach, their work as well as their characters. Händel went to Hamburg because of the significance he saw in Keiser's opera. His contact with the musical organization of the city and the branch of musical art that involved the cantor and organist was accidental, not

sought after, and halfhearted. He became violinist at the opera, and his
friendship with Johann Mattheson, a man
who was to become well versed in the
European aspects of music, probably open-
ed his eyes. Here, Händel and Bach part
with one another at this early stage, at
the very beginning of their artistic ca-
reers. For their ideas about the "end and
purpose" of musical art are fundamentally different. Bach went to Hamburg
for Reinken, the organist. Again this decision reveals destiny, just as does Händel's resolution. The stay at Hamburg
involved Bach still more deeply in the
kind of life his musical goal forced him to
choose.

Unfortunately, no document records
the standard and skill of Bach's organ
playing at this time. He was to be the
master of his age in this field. But the
beginning is obscure. We can take it for

31

granted that he availed himself fully of the training in Böhm's school; he heard Reinken. But we do not know the degree of skill he had himself reached. It cannot have been inconsiderable. The events that followed the short period of Lüneburg make this assumption plausible. Though only eighteen years of age he must have been an organist of some renown.

From 1703 on Bach served as organist at Arnstadt. "Here he began most assiduously to make use of the works of the organists most famous at that time . . . to the advantage of his composition as well as of his playing," says the author of the necrology. Here began the process of elevating German musicianship within its well defined limits. Bach ennobled the office of cantor and organist from within, although the Germans around him were never aware of a process that would give an old office a new dignity. During the period at Arnstadt Bach in fulfilling his official duties came gradually closer to the clear idea about the end and purpose of his music he was shortly to formulate. The cantata "Denn du wirst meine Seele nicht in der Hölle lassen," composed at Arnstadt, is an indication of this aim. It took, however, the meeting with Buxtehude to reach absolute clarity. Bach was determined to visit him; and so he applied for a leave, which was granted for a month in 1705. At the time he arrived at Lübeck the Evening Music (**Abendmusiken**) in the church of St. Mary was at its height. Although these performances had a fairly respectable tradition and, originally, almost entirely the aspect of an entertainment, it was Buxtehude who gave them the final form in which they became famous. The community of Lübeck took part in them, but now for reli-

33

gious edification rather than for reasons
of a musical diversion. Buxtehude gave
the music the character of a religious service. The Protestant liturgy did not actually provide for a service of this kind,
though it came to be associated with the
Sunday Vespers. Tradition had treated
it in an impersonal manner, using music
regardless of the individual composer, as
was the custom in other Protestant services; hymns, chorales, motets were sung.
Buxtehude, however, succeeded in organizing the "service" into a religious
whole, by making his music, to which he
gave the forms of his time, set the tone
throughout. He arranged the Evening
Music as a musical entity, with its own
specific type and of his own making, as
a **drama per musica,** "eine geistliche Opera," an oratorio, but with insertion of
chorales which, in the last analysis, always
represent, or at least invoke, the congre-

34

gation. Thus a unique category of a peculiar church music came to birth, with no authority in past liturgical practice, but with a link to the service of the Vespers and to certain seasons of the church year. The Evening Music took place after the Vespers on the Sundays of Advent, with the exception of the first, and on the last two Trinity Sundays. These evening services had a fairly wide reputation.

Hence Bach was attracted by Buxtehude, not only as the great master of the organ, but also as the inventor of a Protestant service given significance through the music of the individual composer. Bach here experienced church music from an entirely new angle and discovered new possibilities for "organizing" church music as a whole. It even seems that he got a clear view of the "reorganization" he was soon to propose. At all events, never before had he approached the problems of Protestant church music as they were presented at Lübeck. The idea he found realized to a certain extent was this: Buxtehude, that is, an **individual** musician, arranged his own musical concertos for the Evening Music in such a way as to raise the new forms of Italian baroque into an **objective** church music through his appeal to the congregation. This work was complete in itself, based on liturgical tradition and creative in the sense that the music of a single composer produced a new religious service, even though limited in scope, for it comprised merely the five Sundays of the whole year. This form had as its goal the complete organization of the service through music.

The idea of the Protestant church had once more proved productive. The music of the individual composer was called upon to express an idea which must be regarded as the cradle of the Protestant liturgy, the idea of the part played by the congregation in offering the service of prayer and praise. It is not merely the solemnity of elevated language or the intensity of religious feeling that is the primary function of church music. These are only concomitant aspects; they are results perhaps, but certainly not the causes. The true aim is for the individual composer to use his music to organize the service. In the Evening Music of Buxtehude this ideal was realized on a small scale. It is a form of "regulated" church music in which the creative musician weds his work to the objective idea of church and liturgy. If Bach later on saw his particular problem to be the organization of a well-regulated church music, he may have thought of Buxtehude as one of his inspirers. We cannot assume, however, that Bach first learned the very ideal of church

37

music as an entirely new thing from the organist of Lübeck. The "end" of his music was within him, regardless of how clearly he was aware of it. The goal if viewed on a large scale could raise the musician to such greatness as to make him the one and only creator of church music. His music will embody the idea of the whole service. His work must be the symbolic expression of the religious unity that the congregation realizes in the visible form of the service.

Not that Bach was looking for a new frame for his work, for a new organization of the service. The organization was there. But the "organizer," the spokesman of the congregation, should be new. The work will be only the medium; the whole responsibility for the unity of the music of the service is placed upon the individual composer. The only limits are the inner "law" of the artist and the vision he has of the idea of the church. If he should fail in obeying the inner law and in carrying out Luther's idea of the church, he would imperil the service and the musical liturgy as well. There has been no other musician who like Bach possessed the inner force to create church music in the spirit of Luther's church without breaking up the liturgy with an excess of the subjective, and by taking liberties with it as men are wont to do. Again, there has been no other musician whom the problem and the responsibility toward church and liturgy have stirred so deeply as they did Bach. Such a decision and such discoveries constitute the historical significance of Bach's stay at Lübeck and of his meeting with Buxtehude. Of course, the impressions he gained in his study of organ music were by no means of minor importance, since they seem to have rounded out his abilities as an organist and composer of organ music. But the intensive influences that guided his ideas as to an essentially new organization of church music were of far more consequence.

So fully did all this absorb him that he risked overstaying his leave of absence from Arnstadt. He had been granted a month. November passed by, and so did December. It was January 1706 when he once more visited Hamburg for the sake of seeing Reinken; he went to Lüneburg to call on Böhm, and at last arrived at Arnstadt at the end of January 1706. The authorities of the church were utterly indignant over his arbitrary absence. As soon as Bach started his work, he called forth violent protest by his new way of playing the organ; what was really involved, however, was his new style of composition for the organ rather than the mere technique of his performance. Displeasure with his innovations led to formal protests, in the course of which he was severely reminded of his neglect of duty in staying away from his job as he pleased. Finally it came to a break. Bach replied in very concise terms, sure of himself and of his doings: "I was at Lübeck in order to gain an understanding there of one problem and another connected with my art." The reprimand of the clerical authorities called his particular attention to what they took to be evil. Bach, they said, made many peculiar variations in the chorale; he smuggled many foreign tones into the melodies, and thus greatly confused the congregation. It is quite obvious that the new way of giving an individual interpretation to the objective chorale melody, the basis of the musical liturgy, met with apprehension on the part of the authorities. What was to Bach a new religious quality in church music

41

they took to be nothing but a disturbance of the traditional forms. We need not go into the details of the dispute between him and the consistory. It appears that Bach was not at all inclined to compromise; he even seems to have welcomed the controversy as a good reason for resigning his post at Arnstadt. Then follows the exceedingly important phase of his life at Mühlhausen, in 1707.

The cantata begins to take on characteristics that grow more and more essential for his purpose, particularly when Bach develops it around the chorale melody. Like any other category of musical form in the baroque age, the chorale melody has values of its own, its objectivity, its traditional expression. Being an objective category it makes demands of its own which the composer must meet. It is a medium in which the subjective element of the musician must measure itself against the objective qualities of the category. This process underlies the treatment in which the composer recasts the traditional chorale: he breaks it up or expands it; he overlays it with a new surface; he creates a new chorale by ornamenting anew the melody of an old one. That the musician avails himself of the melody at all to build the cantata is purely a matter of structure and composition. The attempt to transform the melody is the result of the demands made by the objective category in the realm of musical form.

But for Bach this attempt springs at the same time from his resolve to interpret a religious reality anew. And here the significance of the text, of the Holy Word, plays its full part, and a distinctively Protestant one. The text stands, as it were, apart from the musical aspects of the melodic structure. Bach strove to create a new melody for the chorale; he exploited the meaning of the text and made it the basis for the melody. Thus he transformed the "traditional" chorale. The process was religiously justified in that he derived it from a relation between the religious meaning of the word and the melody as a new value. In order to be true to the religious sense of the word Bach had to reveal it in music by a closely realistic reproduction. The result was often a melody full of contortions, twists, expansions, brokenness, characteristics that are all significant of Bach's melody, but also indicative of the intensity with which he made his melody the true picture of the religious text. Its meaning was his main concern. Bach's melodies tend generally to realize these features, but they show them with particular clarity in the modified chorales. The power of artistic form emanates

44

from the word which demands musical expression. For Bach attributed to the text the utmost significance; he endeavored to exhaust the religious value of each individual word in accordance with the fundamental Protestant attitude. The deepening of the musical forms by full admission of the individual word imposes upon the melody a rule of progression which cannot be explained by referring it to a melodic structure that has its own proper disposition as well as balance, independent and clear. Bach's characteristic individuality consists in something else. He submits the independent structure of the melody to the test of its adequacy to the necessities of the religious meaning inherent in the text. He interprets the word according to its inner qualities. He took the word as an object in the world of religion. As such, it finds its symbol in the melody. The broken melodic line,

loaded with rhythmic complications, fig-
urative material, ornaments, never as
spontaneous and direct as the Southern
baroque melodies, appears as the very
expression of Bach's religious intensity.

It was typical of the baroque musician
to recognize the categories of musical
form. In this Bach hardly differed from
other contemporary composers. But he
also called upon these categories to symbolize the Holy Word, the object of the
church. Without this any reorganization
of church music in general was impossible.
Bach clung to this idea. He renounced
the way the categories were used and understood in Italy as well as in France.
There they were taken to express man's
bearing in life, his gesture in the world
of appearance. Disregarding the categories as vehicles for expressing the grandiose entertainment of baroque life, Bach
stripped them of the atmosphere in which

they had been brought into existence. Making them responsible to the religious qualities of the sacred word, he combined two diverse elements: one was essentially and intentionally secular, the other made religious by Bach's aim.

While Bach's cantata "Gott ist mein König," composed at the beginning of his activities at Mühlhausen, does not yet reveal all the problems which are to play an essential part in the process of reorganizing church music through the symbolic interpretation of the religious word, the anxiety of his efforts to give the word its due increased because of new influences coming from the movement he had first experienced, although vaguely and immaturely, at Ohrdruf.

For the second time Bach encountered Pietism, and this time in such form as to wrest an inner decision from him. In matters of religious strife Mühlhausen had

47

had abundant experience, which at times had been dearly paid for. The people of the town were able to trace it back to the Reformation when the Anabaptists, the adherents of Thomas Münzer, had started the revolution, political and religious. It was at Mühlhausen that Thomas Münzer was finally executed. Pietism fell here on a soil made fertile by religious conflicts. A violent contention broke out between Pietism and Orthodoxy. Passionate quarrels raged back and forth, from the church of St. Blasius, where Bach was appointed, to the church of St. Mary. On the side of Pietism was the new inwardness of the religious man, the introversion of the individual who makes his own inner self the very source of grace and religious intensity. But this subjective "inwardness" imperilled the forms of religious life as organized and guided by the church. On the other side stood the formalism of Lutheran orthodoxy. Since 1691 Pastor Frohne had advocated for the church of St. Blasius the new intensified religious attitude; from the very start, however, he made it clear that in recognizing the Pietistic movement he did not subscribe to certain disintegrating tendencies, a by-product caused by undisciplined fanatics and seditious hotheads.

When Pastor Georg Christian Eilmar took office at the church of St. Mary, the strife between the two factions broke out. Bach was caught in the very center. Frohne was the pastor of the church where he served as organist. A personal friendship bound him to Eilmar. But this position between the two factions reflected also an inner conflict, in which Bach felt himself drawn to both sides. While at Ohrdruf his youthful experience of Pietism had been prevented from growing, probably by the influences of education and advice in the family where he lived, now his situation at Mühlhausen could no longer save him from internal conflict. No longer could he fall back on the support that the advice of his relatives at Ohrdruf may have afforded. It is quite clear that Bach's nature would keep him aloof from the extremes of an unsteady fanatic. This side of Pietism never endangered him. But, of course, it was not the only side. Pietism as a new intensification of religious experience absorbed him. He was deeply agitated by the ideas to which Pietism gave expression, and the open strife may have increased rather than lessened his agitation. First of all: Pietism was always to him a matter of his own personal religion. He would not escape the decision as to the significance of Pietism for himself and his art. He could perhaps avoid an external decision with regard to his office. In any case, an open declaration of his stand could easily be forced from him. At all times he ran the risk of being brought face to face with such a demand by the authorities. This is, perhaps, another reason for his quick break with his consistory after the return from Lübeck.

At all events, such was the situation: many elements were in favor of the orthodox formalism, whereas his own inclination and his particular attitude toward the religious interpretation of the sacred word in worship and music drove him toward Pietism. The elements in favor of Orthodoxy were: his education and background; his own disposition, which led him to uphold the authority of tradition in general and to abhor all the immoderate exuberance and the revolutionary forces that were bound rashly to destroy the values of the past and the true sense of tradition; and finally, the

51

close link that joined his vocation as an artist and his very position as well to the organization of the orthodox church. There was, furthermore, a factor that set him in definite opposition to Pietism. We know that Pietism favored an extremely puritanical attitude toward the arts and in particular toward music, whose artistic manifestations should have no place in the service of the true Pietist. It may be said that in view of such a principle any further question on this point becomes meaningless or purely theoretical. Actually such questions do not lose their meaning even if we disregard the fact that the authorities at the church of St. Blasius in no way hampered a liberal use of music in the service. But Pietism had now become for Bach an idea which involved his own religious and artistic feelings, quite apart from all its outward implications. We know what books were

in Bach's own library, and that among
them theological works had an outstand-
ing place. We also know the scope of
the Pietistic writings he possessed. A good
many of the works in which the religious
movement found expression were in his
hands: Johann Christian Adami's **Güldene
Aepffel in silbernen Schalen,** Heinrich
Müller's **Göttliche Liebes-Flamme,** Johann Jacob Rambach's **Betrachtung der
Thränen und Seuffzer Jesu Christi,** D.
Philipp Jacob Spener's **Gerechter Eifer
wider das Antichristische Pabstthum,** but
above all the large **Schola Pietatis** by Johann Gerhard. And his Pietistic studies
may very well have made him approach
medieval mysticism; the Sermons of
Tauler were also in his library.

Bach did not allow Pietism to make
itself much felt in his external life. But
he admitted that it exerted its influence
upon his religious ideas of art. And here,

53

indeed, Pietism was of far-reaching consequence. For the Pietist religious intensity came from his attitude toward the evangelical word of the Bible; he discarded the dogmatic meaning which tradition had honored. He devoted himself to the direct meaning of the word. He believed that intimate and spiritual conversation with God will reveal the true and pious sense of the word. He must endeavor to exhaust the inherent secrets of the word in order to find God through it. Whoever fails in humble piety and readiness to believe will not grasp the meaning of the word; to him it will remain closed. The Holy Word, therefore, is not symbolic of the dogma in its formal aspects. The act of interpreting the word depends on the pious intensity of the individual, not at all on the dogmatic sense that men of the past have established and sanctified.

It is Pietism that inspires Bach's attitude toward the religious text that is to be transformed into music. It is Pietism that accounts for his unswerving resolve to approach the concealed meaning of the word, for his devout contemplation of the religious value inherent in the word, and for his anxiety to do full justice to the word whose religious connotations the artistic form must not injure. Whenever he hears the sense God conveys to him through the word, he transmits it directly into music, as the religious element, "operated and operating." This interpretation of the word is equivalent to the creation of new religious realities, and it is the deepest expression of his piety in which he does homage to the meaning of the word as it is revealed to him. Only this Pietistic attitude can help to explain why Bach wanted the musical form, put so often into the most realistic appearance, to be understood as a religious symbol.

If Pietism produced Bach's characteristic approach to the Holy Word, it was also responsible for many a conflict he had to undergo. We can imagine how deeply this conflict affected him, if we take into full consideration that his artistic goal was once and for all church music; that church music called for a reorganization; that Bach was about to make the individual artist alone responsible for the creation of church music so organized that it would interpret the Holy Word in the spirit of Pietism; furthermore, that this goal was possible only within the forms of the orthodox church and could never be reached within Pietism; and finally, that Pietism must have repelled Bach because of its denial of artistic music while it still attracted him for personal religious reasons. And it is this contradictory situation that wrested from him the final decision. There was no escape for the man placed in the midst of antagonistic parties. As a matter of fact, he had no true choice; he did the only thing he could—he left the place. But before leaving Mühlhausen in 1708 he laid down—for all to read—a statement which made clear the very goal of his art.

*A*FTER MÜHLHAUSEN THE
path toward fulfillment seemed free.
Bach's goal was set and his work filled
from within with a new religious intensity. Bach could do what he set out to do
only in the position of an organist and
cantor. At the time when he brought
his work to its decisive phase, he probably did not foresee the consequences
such a position would impose upon him.
He could hardly have thought of the extreme narrowness from which his work

would be doomed to suffer, since such a place had yielded to his forefathers and to his friends a solid foundation for honorable craftsmanship; tradition and experience prevented him from seeing limitation in it or finding fault with it. So he began the organization of church music. He started with organ compositions that should establish the world of new religious realities; they maintained, especially in the chorales and chorale preludes, a close relationship to the Holy Word and to religious emotion. He also began to compose cantatas on a systematic scale; he used texts by Salomo Franck and Erdmann Neumeister; the first perhaps the more intense and devout poet of the two, the latter the more original mind as regards the arrangement of new religious texts to set to music.

We know the ideas Neumeister set forth when he wrote his cantata texts for the purpose of religious intensification. "Having properly performed my official duties on Sundays in the church, I attempted to transform the most significant thoughts that were treated in the sermon into poetic language for my private devotional use. ... Thus these cantatas came to birth." Considered as a musical liturgy, these new texts, essentially musical in their arrangement, offered three elements that contributed to Bach's own musical plans. First: the texts, written for all the Sundays of the church year, took on a liturgical function through their intimate connection with the sermon, which in its turn derived its special characteristics from the Gospel for the day and thus bore out the particular teaching of each Sunday or holy day in the year. Despite the "pious" form of subjective poetry which marked its origin, the cantata became part of the objective liturgy through being linked to the ecclesiastical calendar. There was nothing else in the cantata that made it liturgical. In full conformity with the topic of the sermon, the cantata was placed liturgically between the reading of the Gospel and the sermon.

Secondly, the new poem allowed the individual to penetrate completely the objective sphere of liturgy; this appears a prerequisite for the musician who would make the musical form interpret the religious element in the Pietistic sense. Neumeister regarded his texts as the expression of private piety. He spoke at some length of their poetic characteristics. He laid down the principle that the text of the cantata must express a specific emotion; at that time the various human emotions — "affections" in the baroque terminology — were classified and stereotyped in fixed patterns. Furthermore, being of religious character, it must include a thesis of ethical, or spiritual, import, a "moral." The music will, therefore, have a clear field to express the religious intensity of the affection. Thirdly, the text of the cantata provided for an intimate relation between the musical form and the style of the time. In fact, it is the musical composition of the period that dictated the arrangement of the poem. In Neumeister's own words, a cantata "does not look any different from a piece out of an opera which consists of recitatives and arias." He applied the baroque forms of music to organize the structure of the poem. The musical forms were accepted on the ground that the recitative, the aria, and, above all, the **da capo** aria were common to the Italian baroque cantata and to the opera.

To sum up: from its very origin, the

poem placed strong emphasis on a certain religious feeling of intense but momentary character. The subjective situation, the starting-point for the poetry, shows the cantata to be an outgrowth of the individual's contemplative devotion and piety. It was the intention of the poet to lift man's mind to pious thoughts testifying to the intimate relation of man to God. This, too, implies a free subjective form of religious expression. Despite the many subjective elements in the poem, the cantata nevertheless found its way into the established liturgy. The process which led the poetical content through the moral to the sermon and finally to the Gospel was admitted into the ecclesiastical calendar. But here lies the sole relation between cantata and liturgy. The poetic content, however, is not always a safe ground on which to develop definite and organic forms within the liturgy.

Such a relation between the liturgical order and the poetic content is essentially
weak as well as flexible; and the poet has
too much liberty to make the text a medium of arbitrary expression. As a matter of fact, the degree of safety depended
entirely on the strength with which the
composer realized this relation in each
individual case.

Now the cantata as a species of poetry
never claimed independent poetic value
of its own. On the contrary, the poem
was laid out with a view to the music
from which it derived its structure in
every detail. And this structure was ad-
mittedly of secular origin. Consequently,
if the cantata was to be turned into a
strictly ecclesiastical form, this had to be
done through the music to which it was
set, since the poem was without meaning
in itself.

From the liturgical point of view the

cantata should be more than an accidental contribution to the service. When Bach began to make the cantata the chief medium through which to reorganize church music, he conceived a twofold procedure. He put all the stress on the liturgical character, no matter how weakly and unreliably the poem might have expressed it, in order to attach the form as such indissolubly to the order of the divine service. He began to build up gradually a series of cantata compositions that would meet the requirements of the church calendar throughout the whole year. A great number of German baroque musicians had composed cantatas answering musical needs in the service; most of them took the cantatas merely as a welcome medium with which to bring church music closer to the prevailing secular style. Bach did much more. And here Pietism, or at least the Pietistic idea of the significance inherent in the religious word, makes its artistic influence felt. Bach carried the full meaning of the word into the music; he exploited its religious quality; he made all its secrets speak musically in piety. Through the music the meaning of the word became a new religious reality.

It is in this sense that we have called "the birth of the Church out of the spirit of music" the final achievement of Bach. If the text of the cantata retained its relation to the liturgy—and Bach held this to be indispensable—it would be intensified by the Pietistic interpretation he brought into it. Thus the very character appropriate to each season which the text attempted to keep would obtain its true qualification if the meaning of the text were transformed into a musical symbol. Again Orthodoxy and Pietism confront each other. For the composition of cantatas following the lessons of the calendar through the whole church year derives from orthodox formalism. The devout interpretation of the text, which we have tried to explain, comes from Pietism. This conflict will never leave Bach as long as he pursues his goal. We have anticipated many features in Bach's form of the cantata. In Weimar the scene was set for all he would achieve in this field. It took Leipzig for him to reach the final proportions of the cantata.

With the goal set there seemed to be nothing to hinder Bach from straightforward advance. Everything appeared possible within the musical organization the German town provided. Bach did not doubt that accomplishment would come from his activities as an organist and composer of church music at Weimar. And he was right in not doubting. As yet the question of what place and recognition his music would attain in the rivalry of European countries, did not apparently trouble him. Either he did not realize the importance of such a question, or he avoided it in order to carry out his work faithfully. We have seen that it did not arise at Hamburg, where the musical conditions were very favorable for suggesting it to his mind. Much less did it occur to him at Lübeck. Arnstadt may perhaps have been too limited and too early a stage of his development to make him see the problem. And Mühlhausen brought full concentration on the religious aspects of this work. This is all the more amazing if we think of the contrast between Bach and Händel, who foresaw the question at a strikingly early age and acted accordingly. His inexplicable foresight was reason enough for him to sever his alliance with the musical organizations of the German baroque towns, once and for all. If Bach had not yet encountered the problem, it was his religious goal that kept him from doing so. In working at this task his field of activity was as small as the town where he did his work. And his renown as a composer, even though he declared his intention of reorganizing church music entirely, would hardly reach beyond the field within whose limits he was working. As long as his task controlled him, no doubt could arise, even if Bach were denied in advance the fruits of recognition as a composer and any influential effect upon the vast realms of truly European music. The compositions destined for the church in Germany failed to win acclaim in European circles.

But it is unthinkable that a composer of Bach's proportions would always be able to avoid measuring his own work against all other European music. Nowadays even very minor musicians think in international terms even before they begin really to compose. Sooner or later, Bach was bound to consider his European reputation. This must needs reveal to him the leading part Italy played in the concert of baroque music. As soon as Bach, in his restless search for possibilities of composition, came to strike out and make use of the musical categories of the Italian baroque, he would find what "style" meant among European forms and in the sense of Italian baroque. Then he would realize the true measure of greatness his own work had accomplished in the small town.

Apart from his work for the church he began during his Weimar period to study the Italian style in a more or less systematic way. These studies resulted in compositions which he himself expressly marked **"alla maniera Italiana."** He wrote his concerti after the Italian model of Vival-

di. It has often been said that this new
turn has a very simple explanation: Bach
was proving anew how manifold were his
artistic interests; he never overlooked
any available form of musical expression,
and hence he simply added one more experience. This is quite plausible and in
a way true. Yet it does not hold true
that all Bach's experience of "style" in
music had the same historical meaning
and bearing. The meeting with Buxtehude meant plainly something more than
the acquisition of a certain technical skill.
It would show a great lack of perception
on our part were we to assume, for in-
stance, that Bach's acquaintance with
French music at Celle and his discoveries
at Lübeck possessed the same significance.
His new quest in the field of Italian music has likewise a different historical aspect. To be sure, it began with studies in
style and form. The more systematically

71

he explored the"**maniera**," the more perturbed he must have grown. For the implications latent in all the forms of Italian
music insinuated themselves and made
Bach aware that formal studies involved
at times more than mere manners of
writing.

Bach learned gradually to view his
works in the light of the whole of music.
Here a danger would arise. A temporary
leaning toward a certain manner of com-
posing, or even the systematic imitation
of Italian style, could not imperil his
work. In the Italian forms, however, he
encountered an expansive power and a
predominance over the rest of European
music. He recognized the actual conditions of music as they had been organized
through the work of Italian baroque musicians. These conditions made him feel
that his judgments had been practically
perverted by his constant confinement

within the German town. All the power
with which Italians were directing European music pressed upon him. It made
itself felt through the medium of compositions that were for all purposes and in
all characteristics secular; Italian baroque
music held the secular quality to be the
essence of its being. With its style Italian
music controlled all European music;
Bach's music was limited to a single town.
In its essential quality Italian baroque
was secular; Bach's work was essentially
sacred. In the light of such contrasts, the
maniera Italiana presented itself, indeed,
as far more than a style in the limited
sense. Penetrating into a European range
of music and musical activity, Bach must
have come to doubt whether the work
he had previously composed would ever
attain the European rank to which, of
course, he had a just title.

The recognition of all that Italian style

73

implied had far-reaching consequences. Not only did it act as a corrective element: for the first time Bach availed himself of a European measure and learned to think in European terms. It also raised new hopes that he might himself reach out and seize upon an expansive power like that possessed by the Italian style, so that his own work might be heard throughout Europe. And finally, it caused dissatisfaction with the musical life in the German town. He must have seen clearly now that this type of musical activity would stifle his composition within the walls of the city, rob it of effect in the world at large. The organization of musical life through the **Kantorei,** though of venerable tradition, had grown entirely inadequate to absorb fully the **maniera Italiana** with which Bach was occupied. Did he now visualize the need for a reform of all musical life in Germany?

We do not know. Heinrich Schütz, who found himself face to face with a situation not much different from the one Bach was now beginning to observe, at once drew his conclusions; he adapted the Italian baroque in the style of Monteverdi, but at the same time he recognized that mere transplanting of the new music into the traditional German organizations would not do. And Schütz laid down his ideas about the need of a reform. A man of sixty-three, he published his last work, the **Musicalia ad chorum sacrum, dass ist geistliche Chormusik.** In the preface, grandiose but depressing, he explained that he had failed in his reform, that the German musicians had not followed him, that they had accepted the new style only in part and on a petty scale; but in neglecting a simultaneous reform of the institutions that regulated musical training, they had merely lost the previous craftsmanship the old organization had the advantage of providing. He admonished German musicians to acquire the lost skill through the study of music in the style of the sixteenth century, obsolete but adequate for the **Kantorei** as the traditional school of training.

Bach found that the wide gap between Italian baroque as the prevailing style and German musical life still existed. It is not probable that he desired to bring about a complete reform of German music as a whole. Moreover, with him the baroque epoch was entering upon its last phase. If the problems turned out to be precisely the same as they had been at the beginning of the period, a reform would come too late. Bach himself, toward the end of his life, came to see the dawn of a new age which he probably understood as little as his sons were to understand their own father.

Although a reform of German musical life was apparently far from his thought, the complete grasp of all that the **maniera Italiana** embodied would have brought home to him a revaluation of his work and of German musical art as well. That Bach went out of his way to seize upon the world-wide renown of Italian music for his own sake, cannot be doubted. Strange as it may seem, the more Bach's insight into the actual circumstances of German music grew, the more he, together with all that his work stood for, was imperilled. This might appear a contradiction, since it might seem strange to see danger in his very efforts to gain a far-reaching sphere of influence for his work. But there really was danger. Could Bach's music ever attain its due place in the music of Europe? Was it possible for him to gain a hearing for his work in the countries where Italians had settled the forms through which baroque Europe chiefly expressed itself?

The aim Bach had chosen for his work guided his decisions. There was the problem of reorganizing church music. This task could be carried out only if Bach remained in his position as organist and cantor. Such a position did not allow his works to have an echo in the European world of music. If Bach wanted to break through the narrowness in which his music had to live, he would have to give up his position. Were he to do so, he would betray the aim of his music. The vision of a vast province of action in the world of art was not in keeping with the idea of reforming church music. The two were incompatible. The new goal toward which Bach began to reach out was attractive enough. The prize might be a place in the European repertory, in which Bach's name was completely unknown;

and perhaps a change from the depress-
ingly minor situation of German baroque music might be a secondary reward.
This glimpse into vast regions far beyond the walls of a town, even beyond
the German-speaking countries, held out
a new goal for his whole art. And the
struggle between these two different
goals, church music and the secular greatness of music in Europe, began slowly to
take shape at Weimar while Bach was de-
voting himself to the study of the **maniera Italiana.**

But the choice had to be made. Indeed,
Bach made one of the gravest decisions
of his whole life. He discontinued his
activity at Weimar. In 1717 he began his
new work as Hofkapellmeister of Prince
Leopold of Anhalt-Köthen, the court re-
siding at Köthen. Bach had learned from
the **maniera Italiana** that the culture of
the courts was the medium through

which musical composition would win acclaim in Europe. Perhaps his short visit to Dresden had its share in influencing his decision to leave Weimar. He was determined, unwilling to compromise. The authorities of Weimar did not want him to go; they made efforts to keep him. Bach insisted on leaving. So definitely had he made up his mind that he was ready to go to jail. This imperturbable determination is quite revealing. Behind it stands Bach's vision of a new goal for his music. To attain it was worth many a sacrifice.

In fact, Bach sacrificed things that must have been of the greatest value to him. If he had been known at all hitherto, outside the cities where he worked, it was as an organist that he enjoyed a good name. The only wider reputation he had gained was in the field of organ-playing. Bach gave all this up, at least so far as any

official function was concerned. For Köthen took away from him just this activity. In order to understand this decision
and his new aim fully we should not forget that from the day he left Weimar
Bach never carried on any official activity
as an organist, either at Köthen or later at
Leipzig. He could have had no doubt
that he must renounce his organ-playing
before he made up his mind to go to Köthen. Moreover, Protestantism was of
the reformed branch at the court of Köthen; it was Calvinistic. This also he must
have known well in advance. No uncertainty could ever have entered his mind
that the divine service at the court chapel
would admit of any other sacred music
than the Calvinistic melodies of the
psalms. Such a severe curtailment could
not possibly comply with the imposing
structure of church music that Bach had
originally visualized. There was not a

single factor in the musical situation at Köthen favorable to Bach's art had he really wished to continue working toward his old aim, nothing that lent itself to realizing his plans for reforming church music.

If he nevertheless accepted the position at Köthen, he must have abandoned his first plan, and in doing this, he was swerving from the path that we might have expected him to follow to the very end. In accepting the offer of Duke Leopold, he was embarking upon a new program of musical art. He was rising to the position of **"Kapellmeister,"** the only one that would cast in his way a different musical repertory that would conform to the spirit and style of the time. The **Kapellmeister**, representative of musical activity at the courts, and, as it were, spokesman of a form of life that had made an all-embracing "style" the guide for each and every human expression, was the one status in which the musician could reach out to the powerful manifestations that emanated from the style of nobility. An international reputation could come from such a position, in contrast to that of cantor, which at best led to local significance. Because the aristocratic form of life could be made the vehicle through which to give the work of the artist an international rank, musicians eagerly seized upon every opportunity to obtain a position as **Kapellmeister.** Such a position meant not only a new source of commissions for artistic works, or a pecuniary improvement for the individual artist (sometimes this was not even the case; some posts of **cantor** were actually more lucrative than those of **Kapellmeister**). It meant something intangible that money could not buy, the possibility of European rank as a musician. Händel had a genuine instinct for it, true to the nature of the baroque men, and he made it coincide with the aim of his work.

Bach heeded such an instinct once, and Köthen gave him the chance. He was fully aware of the opportunity the position of **Kapellmeister** afforded for a musician to mould his own destiny. When Leipzig later made an offer, Bach struggled against an inner warning not to return to the post of cantor; he even found it then—in his own words—beneath the dignity of a musician who held his honor in proper regard, to "step down" from the post of **Kapellmeister** to that of **cantor.** In still later years he turned his eyes now and again to the court of Dresden, from which he hoped to get at least the title of **Hofkapellmeister.** Even his return to the old goal that Leipzig brought into sight again, did not make him forget entirely what the position at Köthen had once held up to him as a promise.

The change of "end" in Bach's composition can be seen clearly if we compare the list of works he wrote at Weimar with those he composed at Köthen. The comparison is exceedingly instructive. There are on the one hand the compositions of Weimar. The predominance of sacred works stands out and asserts itself as the contribution to his aim of reforming church music. In the first place there are the church cantatas which originated in collaboration with Neumeister and Franck, about twenty in number. Next, there are the organ compositions, which by their great number as well as by their quality mark the whole Weimar period as a climactic point. (Even the **Orgelbüchlein** he arranged at Köthen draws upon chorale compositions written at Weimar.) The greater part of this organ music is made up of fugues, introduced by preludes or toccatas. There are about forty such compositions if we count the introductory piece and the fugue as one work. Lastly, there are the compositions for harpsichord and clavichord, similar in kind to the Weimar organ music, for the most part preludes, fugues, toccatas, fantasias. In addition to these works there are compositions—studies is perhaps the best term for them—that express the new relation to the ruling **maniera Italiana,** which Prince Johann Ernst, himself a lover of music and a composer as well, inspired and encouraged. It was because of the consequences Bach drew from this inspiration that he left Weimar for Köthen, where his exploration of the **maniera Italiana** went far beyond the scope of "studies."

It is clear from this list of works that it was church music that gave the compositions of the Weimar period their character. The peculiar conditions of Weimar favored the exclusiveness of the artistic standpoint Bach maintained in selecting musical categories each of which contributed its proper share to the ultimate range of a regulated church music. Whether Bach considered that the task he had set himself had been accomplished, in full or in part, must be doubted. The violence with which he severed himself from Weimar, the vision of a new goal which he now made the guide for his artistic work, render it obscure whether all he had done was in his own opinion a first step toward the reorganization of church music, or whether his departure was perhaps an admission of failure in the face of the insurmountable obstacles between his task and the general spirit of the times. At all events, the further Bach carried his religious work, the more bitter grew the conflicts with the authorities during each of the periods in which he devoted himself to this task.

On the other hand we have the list of works composed at Köthen. Its character is just as exclusive as that of Weimar. During the six years of his activity at the court, from 1717 to 1723, Bach neglected the church cantata entirely, and this neglect came abruptly. There are, in fact, only two that can, with certainty, be assigned to the Köthen period, and these are dedicatory works. Criticism of style may well succeed in relating one cantata or another to this period. But any new discovery would scarcely change the picture. With regard to organ compositions also, the situation is reversed from what it had been at Weimar. The composition of only one work is established, the great Prelude (Fantasia) and Fugue in G minor, written in 1720. Indeed, the whole list points to another origin and springs neither from the liturgical cantata, nor from the religious organ composition, nor from church music at all.

Again, we find quite a number of works for keyboard instruments. But here too Bach has changed plan and purpose, although the construction of preludes, fugues, fantasias, and toccatas still occupies his interest. First and foremost, however, the special meaning and technique of playing a keyboard instrument attracted him for purposes of instruction. With this end clearly in view he composed the **Clavier Büchlein** for his son Wilhelm Friedemann (1720), the **Noten Büchlein** for his second wife, Anna Magdalena (1721 and 1725), the first part of the **Wohltemperirte Clavier** (1722), the two-part inventions as well as the three-part symphonies which he combined into a special collection after the **Clavier Büchlein** for Wilhelm Friedemann. Next to

these works, which became the imperish-
able documents of "house music" on
the highest level of craftsmanship, he was
attracted by the suite, that species of
composition which so adequately reflected the gallant and cultivated taste of
baroque life. In the field of keyboard
music his efforts to cope with the structure and stylized expressiveness of the suite
resulted in the collection of the English
and French suites (1722/23). It has re-
cently been found quite probable that the
"English" suites derive their surprising
name from a relation to Händel's suites
of 1720, with which Bach's collection has,
among other things, the opening in A
major in common. The English suites
may consequently have been written in
1721, owing the free and "unreflective"
manifestation in which Händel's work
abounds to a certain imitation of his
style; at least this character seems to per-

tain more to the English than to the French suites.

A large part of the Köthen repertory is given to various forms of chamber music. Here, the **maniera Italiana** led Bach to adopt all the categories of composition used in performances in the "camera," at court. The repertory, then, shows the baroque sonata in a great variety of media. The solo sonata is represented by compositions for the violin, for the gamba, for violin and harpsichord, for flute and thoroughbass; there are sonatas for two violins, for two flutes with **basso continuo,** there is the sonata for violin, flute and thoroughbass in G major. Some of these sonatas, remarkably instructive, have Bach's own realization of the thoroughbass. And, finally, there come the compositions for the orchestra. The suite appears now as an overture with the orchestra as its medium of performance;

the list of works shows also the three concerti for violin and orchestra and the D minor concerto for two violins and orchestra; and above all the Brandenburg Concerti.

Instrumental works, for ensemble or keyboard, predominate in the repertory of Köthen, as did church music among the compositions written at Weimar. The change is sudden; it also is complete. Its significance cannot really be mistaken. Bach has moved out of the sphere of church music; he is building up a stock of compositions, new in the total range of his works; he is aiming at a sphere of art that Italian baroque had more and more successfully made the extreme opposite of church music, the realm of chamber music, indissolubly linked to the life of the court. Bach had foreseen all this. His foresight had led him to make his choice. It is utterly inappropriate to assume that

it was merely the particular circumstances he encountered at Köthen that turned
his work in a new direction. Actually,
baroque music was always bound up with
the objective situation in which it arose.
For the local conditions to exert their
influence upon the character of a musical
work is, throughout the period and in
every country, quite natural. This, however, was not at all open to question
when Bach changed Weimar for Köthen.
His foresight of all that was to come: the
want of any opportunity to compose for
the church, the loss of service as an organist; these stand against the materalistic
explanation which would make the greatest work of musical art merely an outgrowth of circumstances without ever
allowing for a decision made by the artist
himself, and without taking into account
the significance the work had for the
composer which the historian must at-

tempt to discover. How should the principal change in the repertory of Köthen be explained if we must discard the mere accident of circumstances as its sole reason? What else is there to be said if we cannot satisfy ourselves with the dry-as-dust statement of the factual change? What else but that Bach has set up a new goal for his art, that he has given up his former aim? We cannot escape the reasons that lie deep in the composer's attitude, which his repertory reflects in the nature of the compositions included, perhaps more clearly than in any other factor.

This shift in repertory was in conformity with an internal change in Bach's work. The struggle for repute in the ranks of European musicians, for a coincidence between his work and the spirit of the times, together with the desire to lift German music out of a narrowness that tradition had rendered unavoidable, bestows upon the period of Köthen momentous fascination. Bach begins to speak a European language in adopting the various species of instrumental music; and he makes the expressions of the life of the court his servants, hoping that their international quality will penetrate his work and abide to the end, so that the order of baroque nobility throughout the world may recognize that in them its own tones are resounding. Surely the new goal was no less worthy than the first. Indeed, the works of Köthen seem to abound lavishly with the life of the world and all its sweeping might. There is something common to all the compositions Bach wrote at Köthen, a particular tone almost unmistakable to recognize. They show Bach intent upon massive effects, fullness of sound, rhythms of an unimpeded vitality, upon characteristics by means of which many articles of the baroque age in all the arts expressed the harmony and order of the world, as well as the gesture of the law of baroque life.

Bach often appears to us as "introspective" or, better, as a discoverer of the constructive possibilities latent in objective and movable tones; he knows these "mathematical" secrets inherent in sound; he appears as a magician who understands how to take the soundings of the aptitude of tones to be combined one with another; this is a secret whose depth few of his contemporaries had penetrated. But here at Köthen there is still another Bach, less involved in the mysterious nature of tones as objects of the given world. Never again did Bach come out with so powerful a manifestation of vitality, never was he so certain of the sovereign gesture as an expression of life, never so full of self-assertion and of a natural demand for mastery, as in the grandiose scale of the Brandenburg concerti. Neither was he ever so free from the narrowness of the German burgher as in the Köthen period. Indeed, his work seems here to have absorbed the world tone which the baroque musicians strove to realize. While hitherto one element or another of his composition had always been bound to some tradition of the narrow German city, the European tone he strikes at Köthen is nowhere impaired by any such limitation. Is it then to be wondered at that Bach in years to come looked back upon Köthen as the happiest time of his life even from a personal point of view? The inner freedom he gained for his art, the contact with the whole of European music he thought he had found for his composition, the power the universal spirit of baroque life granted, the feeling of being in concord with the times, the strength that the communication with circumstances on a large scale and broader view afforded; all this eased his way of life and bestowed upon his work a convincing, spontaneous sweep, not always present in his composition. Oftener his music stirs men more through its deeply contemplative nature, through the "melancholia ingenii." The masterly directness, however, that emanates from the work of Köthen Bach never again attained. Händel commanded it as a bountiful gift of nature. Bach had to struggle for it; never did it come naturally to him; and only once did he fully succeed in casting off the inhibitions a cumbrous tradition made him bear.

Although the Köthen work did not make itself felt within European music as a whole—this was its true "end," foreseen or hoped for—its effect was not lost in a vacuum as was the case of Bach's other compositions. An astounding historical process springs from the work of Köthen. It is remarkable that Bach's sons should have taken up this work as the very starting-point for their own advance. They certainly neglected the later work, that of Leipzig, as much as all their other contemporaries did; they understood it as little as everyone else; they acted as though the work of Leipzig did not exist. But they seized upon the work of Köthen, whose spirit they followed and felt to be part of their own. They understood the direct address of this work to the European whole to be in keeping with the times. Bach's sons took it up and carried on from there, particularly Carl Philipp Emmanuel. It matters not what changes they were to bring into the message of Köthen; their primary understanding secured a direct line of development. Thus the Köthen Bach entrusted a heritage to the younger generation. Thus was the success, not an unconditional one and certainly not one that fulfilled all expectations. If the Köthen work did not really become part of Europe's music, at least it hammered out a link with which to hold old and young together. Thus Bach's efforts to give his composition a European message were not altogether in vain, even if the boundaries of Germany set the limit to the message.

Bach wrote in later years to one of his friends that he highly esteemed Prince Leopold of Köthen, both as lover of music and as connoisseur, and that he had hoped he could live and work at his court for the rest of his life. He was denied the satisfaction of doing so. Although he moved into an entirely new sphere of activities when he went to Köthen, he could not cut off his past as completely as he hoped to. That is to say, his reputa-

55321

tion as an organist had grown so great that it now made certain demands upon him. Throughout the period of Köthen he was continually invited to test organs in nearby churches. During the early 'twenties certain occasions must have reminded him strongly of his previous task. At least the past frequently made itself felt through his close relations with organists. When the famous position of organist at St. Jacobi at Hamburg became vacant, the church where Neumeister was pastor, Bach was considered, Neumeister being the most ardent advocate of the call. But nothing came of it, and an organist far inferior to Bach was preferred. The decision disappointed Neumeister so deeply that he gave vent to his anger publicly in a sermon. These things may amount to no more than inconsequential interludes; but they must have sounded vivid enough to recall to Bach's mind the ideas he had entertained about the state of church music. His reputation as an organist did not allow sacred music to fall into complete oblivion. These interludes may have come like admonitions. They could in the long run accumulate enough weight to confuse the task Bach was accomplishing at Köthen. It also seems that a new turn of affairs at the court of Köthen may have lessened the readiness of the prince to patronize music. At any rate, Bach himself makes mention, though not altogether convincingly, of this change. Prince Leopold had married in 1722. And Bach wrote: "things seem to assume an appearance as though the musical inclination of the prince would grow somewhat lukewarm, since the new princess appears to be uninspired by the Muses"; an "amusa" she is said to have been. Be this as it may, Bach's activity at Köthen came to an end in 1723.

HEN CAME LEIPZIG. IT
made the period of Köthen one of tran-
sition. The stage was set for the most
tragic epoch of Bach's life, and the reason for the tragedy was that a fusion between German musical style and European
music had never taken place. Bach return-
ed to his first aim; it was to become his
last. The possibility of reconciling through
his own work the music of Germany with
the musical spirit of the times seemed to have vanished forever. Bach

revived the musical aim he had expressed in the document of Mühlhausen in 1708. If some works composed during the last year at Köthen show a new religious turn, they can perhaps be taken to indicate a reawakening of the old aim. It was in feeling his way back to the reorganization of a well-regulated church music that he first came in contact with Leipzig, especially through the St. John Passion, written for Leipzig and performed there. But any attempt to start the reorganization anew would of necessity lead him back into the narrowness of the cantor's function. For nothing had changed the fact that only in this position could he make a new and final effort toward his goal. The question became acute when the vacant post of cantor at St. Thomas's called for an appointment in 1722, the year of Kuhnau's death. At first, Bach did not apply for the position. It is well known that the council of the city did not consider Bach at all. Since the distinction of the post required the careful election "of a famous man," the council looked around for a musician thus qualified. Hence they negotiated first with the "world-renowned" Telemann, musical director at Hamburg. After failure to come to terms with him, Christoph Graupner, Hofkapellmeister at Darmstadt, was next in line. It is of great significance that neither of these men, regarded as really famous, held the position of cantor, although the council should, logically at least, have sought for a musician distinguished in this office; all the more as the formula of appointment expressly demanded that the musician to be installed should not compose church music that would sound like an opera. Despite the cantatas Graupner wrote, he can hardly be imagined as the right person to meet such a demand; and even the versatile and prolific Telemann does not appear to have been particularly fitted for the position, at least not as a result of his activity at Hamburg, since it was there that he had composed most of his operas.

The name of Bach, then, entered the discussion only after failure with both Telemann and Graupner. This fact has, historically speaking, a double significance; on the one hand for the extent of Bach's fame within Germany, and on the other for the way in which a musician's fame grew—surely, not in the position of cantor. The council of Leipzig significantly did not look among the cantors to find a man to occupy the post of cantor. Neither did Bach consider the post most desirable; he hesitated to accept the appointment when it came; he seems to have been fully aware of the limitations it would place again on the recognition of his work. We have already remarked that he thought "at first it could not at all comport with his dignity to become a cantor after being a Capellmeister." With the old goal probably in view, he finally resolved "to step down." And he said of Leipzig: "this post has been pictured to me so favorably that I finally took the risk in the name of God."

Gräfenhahn published a "Rede der Musik" in 1754. In an important passage he speaks of German musicians, mentioning only Händel and Telemann. Bach is not included, naturally because of his lack of recognition. The editor of Gräfenhahn's work, however, felt that he should complete the list of German musicians, "to the honor of the German nation," and he added first the name of Hasse, then that of Graun, and in the third place Bach, who immediately precedes musicians such as Weise, Pantalon,

Heinichen, Quantz, Pisendel, Stölzel, Bümmler, all of them "great masters according to their kind." This reflects precisely what Germans thought of Bach's importance for German music.

After 1723, when the period of Leipzig began, Bach became more and more isolated. It is, however, not at all true that this growing isolation resulted from a certain quality of style in his music, in which it might be supposed that he was reaching out far beyond his own time in anticipation of the future. Bach's music had no bearing on the time to come. It fulfilled itself entirely within the baroque, in retrospect rather than in prophecy; this holds true even though finally the greatness of his composition has marked his work with that timelessness in which all great works of any period join each other.

Bach's isolation was his tragic destiny

in history, bound up with his ideas for church music. When he took up this task again, it meant, as it were, a "home-coming": the mature Bach was returning to what he had once in his youth deemed final. This last vision of his goal came with stirring suddenness. Bach now held fast to it, with a determination from which an almost incredible productivity emerged. Within about eleven years, from 1723 to 1734, he composed approximately a hundred cantatas, the Magnificat, Sanctus, chorales, motets, the St. Matthew Passion, the Christmas Oratorio, and the B minor Mass, completed in 1738. As it were on the borderline between the period of Köthen and that of Leipzig stands the St. John Passion. By their elimination from the liturgy Bach's motets have merely maintained their old position as occasional works; the few motets he did write are nearly all composi-

tions intended for funerals. Here again
we have an extremely interesting fact
indicative of the conflicting factors in
German baroque music. For the cantor
was now deprived of one of his oldest
functions, the composition of motets.
Instead of being discarded altogether,
they were still kept in the Protestant service. Their liturgical place was at the beginning of the service. Since the cantor
was no longer obliged to write new motets, the choir of St. Thomas selected the
works for this liturgical purpose from
the **Florilegium Portense** of Bodenschatz,
a collection of motets whose sixteenth-
century musical style was completely an-
tiquated.

With his return to the religious task,
Bach found his last form. If we now
speak of a "style of Bach," we usually
think of the work that originated at Leipzig, as though the last manifestations of

his art summarized all he had been or could ever have been. While he was finding the final structure for his composition, the conflict with the tendencies of his time was growing gradually more intense. At length he succeeded in attaining the goal he had set himself. Yet success brought him complete loneliness as an artist; at the end, he was alone in fact. It was the great tragedy of his musicianship that at the close of his life he could say that he had accomplished what he set out to achieve. But his accomplishment echoed in a vacuum. This was a momentous catastrophe, not only for Bach but for the whole ideal of his work. His most mature compositions, significant of his later style, won no acclaim in their own time. This tragedy of his work could well be said to amount to a catastrophe for the whole musical situation in the middle of the eighteenth century, and,

111

indeed, a far-sighted contemporary did say so. Any attempt to remedy the generally catastrophic situation of music drove Bach still further away from his own contemporaries. We have seen that his "successors," his sons, Carl Philipp Emmanuel in particular, and the so-called "early classics" turned to the works of Weimar and Köthen, when and if they maintained any link with Bach. Thus the cantor of St. Thomas's was left in increasing loneliness such as few have known. The language of the Leipzig Bach was never heard; and many a man who knew Bach's name thought he had grown silent altogther. Indeed, there are tragic undertones when, in conversation among friends and relatives, Bach was spoken of as the "old wig of Leipzig." Yet the old Bach was right when he considered his Leipzig works, the greatest he ever wrote, to have reached the state of fulfillment.

112

Quite naturally with the passing of the years he grew more and more irritable, peculiar, even stubborn and inaccessible. He would not compromise in any matter of principle even though in his relations with the authorities he bent the bow until it broke. He knew his task could not be tampered with; but he probably knew also that the gap between his work and the times was widening year by year. The Leipzig authorities spoke of the "incorrigible" Bach when they were confronted with this unwillingness to compromise. The struggle for the very goal of his music became more bitter every year. This can be seen in numerous documents. Of great importance in this respect is his **Brief, but utterly necessary outline of a well-regulated church music, with some additional unprejudiced consideration of its decline** of 1730. Four years later, with the appointment of Johann August Ernesti, who represented "enlightened rationalism," as the Rector of St. Thomas's, the old principle of the school, "to guide the students through the euphony of music to the contemplation of the divine," was discarded. The "Enlightenment" with which the new generation disintegrated religion confronted Bach from within as well as from without. His younger contemporaries began to shake their heads over what the "old wig" was doing at Leipzig. Attacks were even forthcoming on his music, on his "unnatural" style. The "pompous and confused character robs his compositions of the natural, and too great artificiality obscures their beauty." The attitude of the enlightened rationalist toward nature in art is clearly revealed in this criticism. The Leipzig Bach is still recognized as a great organist, but beyond that the younger men would not go. "This great man," they say, "has in no way explored the 'sciences' [humanities], the knowledge of which should be required from a learned composer." An odd thing to say of Bach of all men! But such was the injustice the enlightened younger generation inflicted upon the cantor of Leipzig if they happened to notice him at all. The angry disputes between Bach and the authorities of school and church, which are all set forth in lengthy documents, disputes the effects of which beclouded nearly the entire period of Leipzig, were not merely a controversy between individuals. They implied a collision between two times. It was this that sharpened the temper of everyone involved; and it was for this reason that reconciliation was impossible. The spirit of the Enlightenment admitted no understanding of Bach's task, and made the old style of his Leipzig work subject to criticism and neglect.

115

When later times brought an historical revival of Bach, the discovery—such it was in fact—that called the works into life for the first time began with the Leipzig compositions. Since the compositions of Weimar and Köthen had been to some extent transmitted to the younger generation, it was not necessary to make them accessible anew. They had already played their historical rôle through their influence on younger musicians. But with the Leipzig work the situation was different. There, everything had been forgotten. The Romantics, therefore, revived that part of Bach's work with which the historical connection no longer existed, if it ever had. Only then did we come to know what the particular style of Bach means in its essential character and climactic accomplishment. Ever since, when we speak of the "style of Bach," we mean that of Leipzig.

Although this later work accomplished at Leipzig has all the distinguishing marks of an unbroken unity, Bach himself, filled with boundless anger at the unsurpassable lack of understanding on the part of the authorities, often looked with envy as well as anguish toward the splendor of the court music at Dresden, where musical affairs were conducted in a way which Bach held up as an example to his superiors at Leipzig. His experience at Köthen had shown him the values of a "Hofkapellmeister." About the middle of his Leipzig period, in 1733, the year of the death of Augustus the Strong, he made contact with the court of Dresden. He strove to obtain an appointment there as Hofkapellmeister; and he lent his endeavor weight with a work he intended to dedicate to Augustus III; together with the St. Matthew Passion it now belongs to his greatest works. The cantata, which he had made the most substantial part of the Protestant liturgy, was entirely inappropriate for the Catholic court at Dresden. Hence the Protestant Bach wrote for a Catholic environment the B minor Mass for which he used, at least in part, some of his cantatas previously composed and now rearranged for the Latin text of the mass. It took him many an effort to extract a court "Predicate" from the Prince Elector. He set amazingly great store by this mark of distinction, which was nothing but a title. Later, the title was given him. He never forgot thereafter to lay the greatest stress upon the rank of Hofkapellmeister. His true position, however, was in no way affected; the title changed nothing. Because of the tension that existed between him and the authorities, he took some of his duties lightly in later years, as letters prove. He often went away without the request for permission he was required to submit whenever he planned a journey. He played the organ here and there with unmatched virtuosity. He made tests of organs, visited his sons and tried to keep up his relations with Dresden by fulfilling "obligations" he imagined himself under as Hofkapellmeister. The last church cantatas, among them "Du Friedefürst, Herr Jesu Christ," were completed in 1744 and 1745. Thereafter, organ composition came back into the foreground. This, too, was a return to the beginning. The last years closed the circle. His life ended, in 1750, with what had once started his artistic work, organ music.

E SHALL NOT FULLY comprehend the whole greatness of Bach's work unless we have made clear its historical significance, which first finds far-reaching expression at Mühlhausen. The Leipzig years brought a complete break with his times. The sacred music of Leipzig was given a form beyond any of the tendencies the age produced. The style of the Leipzig Bach spoke neither to his times nor out of his times. His contemporaries were no longer stirred by it. After going to Leipzig, Bach preserved his work from any inner change. However flexible he may have been in his youth, in his later years he hardened himself against change, so far as the principal aim of his composition was concerned. Not that he had become incapable of development. He had reached the goal. His work grew to be so unapproachably compact and uniform that we perceive only its exceptional and complete independence, without being especially aware of any essential relation to the age of the Enlightenment. It appears as though Bach had shut out all intercourse with his times. This timelessness was the result not only of the greatness of his work; it emanated also from the religious goal of his art, which could only be realized in the inescapable narrowness of the sphere of his activity.

Bach spoke apart from the spirit of the

age, although he was intent upon guiding it. Händel, on the other hand, was seized with the spirit of the times, of which he was at once servant and master. Händel created his work in accordance with this spirit, Bach ran counter to it. Händel was rooted in the effective and great associations of his time. Bach had once searched for them, but toward the end of his life he came to realize that in fact he had never found them. Händel reached his greatness within the times in which he lived, and through them, Bach against them. Hence Bach's "timelessness" made it possible—and this is true also from the historical point of view—to link the spirit of his work to other epochs which believed themselves closer to its essential aim than the age in which he lived. At times the steadiness of his character has been compared with that of the men of the Reformation; at times the form of his life has been found more akin to the men of the seventeenth century. Dilthey once said that the whole structure of his character belonged to the seventeenth century, when men were more staunch than Bach's own contemporaries; that, furthermore, "subjection to religion established his being," since his essential character rested upon "an unshakable religious feeling.... He seems to have known religious poetry only in connection with the chorale and related lyrics. Consequently, he did not move his own contemporaries to the measure of his genius."

We have attempted to set forth the general characteristics of Bach as well as the essentials of his work by searching for his historical significance. We cannot consider him anything but Protestant. The power and effect of his work lies, indeed, within Protestantism. But the form in which he expressed himself as a Protestant did not derive from his own times; it originated in sharp opposition to them, and he was powerless to force the Protestantism of his making upon the world around him. Just as the style of his later works developed apart from his own contemporaries, so the form of his Protestant religion had likewise no share in the prevailing ideas of the time. We should like to formulate this historical destiny through a parallel: Bach was driven into seclusion as an **artist**, and consequently also as a **Protestant**; or, he came to endure **religious** isolation, and consequently also that of his **art**.

The age, which Bach expected to accept his vision of a complete reform of church music, was wholly incapable of seeing its character and necessity. The rationalists attacked traditional religion from all sides, and they quickly found their way out of the church. One aspect of religion, individual religious feeling taken as the necessary intensive quality of religion, was preserved in part by Pietism. But this was not without grave peril; for it gave the individual an opportunity to seek religious expression outside the traditional church. Orthodoxy opposed this movement with the whole power of the canonical organization, which vindicated its claim to mold the religious life through dogma and tradition. Against this the Pietist maintained that the life of the church had declined to the mere administration of externals, completely subject to organization, which should never be allowed to assume more importance than the personal value of religion for which the individual must be held responsible. Bach was born into a time that did not seem equal to the task of eliminating the perilous elements in these movements. It now became possible to carry on religious life entirely outside the formal institution of the church.

It is for such reasons that church music as a whole necessarily declined, all the more since the leading musical style of the period took its rise quite apart from all sacred music. Bach was aware of the decline as no other musician of his day. In the existing state of the church he saw the urgent need for reform, which would effect a complete reorganization of the music in the Protestant service. His religious conscience as well as the weight of his religious responsibilities led Bach to this artistic task. He saw it always as directly bound up with the liturgy, since no musical reform could have any effect unless music and liturgy were taken as a unity. Pietism, however, had struck so hard a blow against the connections of music with liturgy as to preclude any reform of church music within its sphere.

A genuine success might be expected only if the religious intensity of Pietism and the existing forms of the traditional liturgy could be brought together. Bach carried into his task the impetus that came from Pietism toward intensifying the religious life. This religious intensity, awakened in him by Spener and Tauler, set a new goal for the reform.

The question has often been raised as to the precise nature of this reorganization of musical liturgy. That a musician had arisen who succeeded in completing the music for the cult by furnishing cantatas for all the services of the year; one capable of creating music as an outgrowth of his own religious conscience; one religiously intense and able to stir the innermost spirit of man in religious expression; all this has the mark of highest distinction. But it does not suffice to answer the question fully. For other musicians in

Bach's time also wrote cantatas, many of them even a series to cover the whole church year. But none of them was at one and the same time innovator and conserver in the spirit of the Protestant church.

"By leading the whole influence of the life of man's soul into a typical expression either of the poetic word or of music, a certain period comes to full awareness of its own religious feeling. Now, from the works of religious poets and musicians there are forthcoming intensities of the religious life which would otherwise slumber in the inscrutable depth of the human soul. The great epoch of the Protestant religion possessed such a knowledge of its own fullness and immeasurable profundity in the church chorale, in the sermon, above all, however, in religious music." Dilthey has thus expressed the way in which he understood the religious music of Johann Sebastian Bach.

128

Music has raised "the Protestant religion, as it were, to eternity." Bach did this for the Lutheran religion. Is such an appraisal, then, the ultimate analysis of the ideal of his work, the ultimate interpretation of musical form in the realm of the church? Are there perhaps no other words to measure the immeasurable than those of religious feeling and intensity, whose vagueness is unbounded?

The baroque brought into music the motions of man's soul, the dynamics of the various states of the soul most profoundly and comprehensively expounded by Descartes and Mersenne. The musician had to understand this dynamics as the rhythm of the passions in human life. The passion of man, man himself became the powerful tenor upon which the composition of all baroque music had been built since the time when Claudio Monteverdi expressly refused to present inanimate matter unrelated to man, and proposed that man, his passion and his suffering, should be the subject-matter of art. Musicians thereafter embarked upon excited disputes about the matter; they did not cease to discuss the human affections to be expressed through musical composition.

When Bach began his work, he could draw on a fairly large range of forms and expressions established as tradition. He transformed human affection—in the baroque sense of the term—into a **religious reality of the church.** Pietism kindled in him, as well as in others, the states and passions of the soul as religious experiences. These must now be harmonized with the idea of the church, that is, within the congregation. Only thus could the idea of the church be expected to live. Church music, to spring from and flow back into the congregation, must be reorganized upon a sure foundation; for this only the most general all-embracing principle of art would suffice. This general principle should comprise all members of the congregation; and it should be comprehended by all of them as well. Furthermore, it should be one with the subject-matter of art in general and of musical composition in particular. For Bach never intended to depart from the musical language of the period in the manner of a revolutionary who would destroy tradition; he did not aim at breaking with his times; his work conformed entirely to the baroque style however far he expanded its possibilities.

Hence, the thought to be expressed in each particular composition, and the medium through which to renew church music in keeping with the idea of the church, must be brought into complete unity. This unity could be attained only

131

through **affection,** the crucial element in the life of baroque man. For it is affection that has both a human and a musical basis; it can also be given religious significance. Affection, then, serves to organize the structure of the musical liturgy; it animates the individual musical work. Bach spiritualized the affections and made of them musical elements in the life of the church. That is to say, he imparted to them qualities that reflected the aspirations of the congregation and in which it could join with its own unbroken religious expression. Bach was not alone in looking upon affection as a phenomenon of art and composition; others had done so before him. It was his peculiar contribution that he gave it its place within the church. He understood it as something through which the religious intensity of the whole congregation might be expressed. He chose it as the

132

sign and symbol for the benefit of the congregation. He took it as the Lutheran "confessio."

Bach also recognized the power of affection in the truly artistic sense. Affection was to the man of the baroque age perhaps the deepest secret of life. It was like an inexhaustible force always striving from within outward to find expression in human gestures; we are not able to say whence it comes, or what it is that continually renews it. This force retained its mysterious character in the music of the baroque. Men of the age were spontaneous in their understanding of the affections, because they felt in themselves their power. They thought of them as the various states through which man manifests his life in relation to the world. The succession of these states would form a dynamic rhythm rising and falling like a tide through his whole being, stirring body and soul alike. It is this rhythm that controlled the baroque conception of art.

Bach laid hold upon this property of the affections to move the whole being of man and brought it to bear upon the feeling of the congregation. Any affection should appeal to the congregation as a whole. The church, the symbol of the congregation, is the court of last resort to pass upon the religious value of the affections. Bach was, accordingly, in a position to remold the chorales along the same lines. The alterations he made in the traditional melodies are significant of this. He created a whole world of unchanging forms for certain ideas—mental and emotional images. We often speak of his "motives" or "symbols." Among these, his symbol for Jesus Christ, which he carries throughout his whole work, is the strongest in religious intensity and most prominent among the symbolic expressions of the congregation. Bach did not create such categories of types, motives and symbols to the exclusive end of a direct appeal through musical language; he created them in the service of the congregation. The affections obtained their lasting, symbolic forms in music, just as the sacred word retained its unalterable meaning. They were "confessions" of timeless values. Through them Bach accomplished the reorganization of Protestant church music. With them he proclaimed to a time devoid of understanding "the birth of the Church out of the spirit of music."